STUDENT BOOK

T0385972

Laura Miller • Tessa Lochowski
Series advisor: David Nunan

Pearson Education Limited
Edinburgh Gate
Harlow
Essex CM20 2JE
England
and Associated Companies throughout the world.

Poptropica English

© Pearson Education Limited 2015

Based on the work of Tessa Lochowski

The rights of Laura Miller and Tessa Lochowski to be identified as authors of this work have been asserted by them in accordance with the Copyright, Designs and Patents Act 1988.

Stories on pages 16, 26, 38, 48, 60, 70, 82, and 92 by Catherine Prentice. The rights of Catherine Prentice to be identified as author of this work have been asserted by her in accordance with the Copyright, Designs and Patents Act 1988.

Phonics syllabus and activities by Rachel Wilson

Editorial and project management by hyphen

First published 2015
Twenty fourth impression 2024

ISBN: 978-1-292-09081-8

Set in Fiendstar 17/21pt

Printed in Slovakia by Neografia

Illustrators: Adam Clay, Leo Cultura, Joelle Dreidemy (Bright Agency), Tom Heard (Bright Agency), Andrew Hennessey, Marek Jagucki, Sue King, Stephanine Lau, Daniel Limon (Beehive Illustration), Katie McDee, Bill Mcguire (Shannon Associates), Baz Rowell (Beehive Illustration), Jackie Stafford, Olimpia Wong, Teddy Wong and Yam Wai Lun

Picture Credits: The Publishers would like to thank the following for their kind permission to reproduce their photographs: (Key: b-bottom; c-center, l-left; r-right; t-top)
123RF.com: 73c (Flowers), 86tc/3, 90cl/5, 94tl, Frank Bach 62bc/b, Marie Ann Daloia 62br/c, Jose Manuel Gelpi Diaz 85cr (Boy), Gekaskr 96c/b, Michael Gray 109cl, Dzianis Miraniuk 86c/9, Nytumbleweeds 40cr, Paffy 111tl/1, Pat138241 42br, Marina Scurupii 40br/4, Rohit Seth 37br, 109c, Sirikorn Thamniyom 111cl/3, Leah-Anne Thompson 90tc/2, Waldru 109tr/a, Tracy Whiteside 43b; **Alamy Images:** Vincent Abbey 41cl (Balloon dog), Jeffrey Blackler 73cl, Paul Brown 108c, Nick Fielding 41tc (Sunflowers), Johner Images 72br/a, Alistair Laming 72tr; **Brand X Pictures:** Burke Triolo Productions. 84bc/7, 86tc/2; **Comstock Images:** 68cr/8; **Datacraft Co Ltd:** 72br/b; **Digital Stock:** 62bl/a, 95cl; **Eyewire:** 29c (Piano); **Fotolia.com:** Alex555 81c (Cake), Asbtkb 64cl/d, Darren Baker 81bc, Viktor Chinkoff 64cl/a, Coloures-pic 42bl, Antonio Diaz 30br, D. Fabri 62cr/c, Elisabetta Figus 90tl/1, Vadim Gnidash 18tc (Fish), Marina Ignatova 94cr/4, 94bl/a, Kai 85c (Chocolate), Markus Mainka 31br, Mast3r 107br, Mgkuijpers 109tr/b, Monkey Business 42c (b), Piotr Pawinski 68tc/2, Julija Sapic 63c (Rabbits), Satori 41c (Collage), Sentello 51tc (Girl), SergiyN 21bl, 30bl, 74bl, L. Shat 80tr/6, 80c (Orange juice), Soleg 40tc, Speedfighter 110tc/b, StarJumper 18bl (Flamingo), Stockphoto-graf 80tc/5, 80c (Ice cream), Syda Productions 106br, Tobago77 51tc (Shower), WavebreakmediaMicro 109tl, Womue 84br/8; **Getty Images:** Zsolt Biczo 84tl, Digital Vision 28cr, Albrecht Durer 41c (Rhinoceros), Fotografia Basica 40tr, Fuse 84tr, istock 40c, 40bl/1, Jupiter Images 106cr, Oliver Lang 108cr, SA2RN 84cl, Jonathan Utz 108cl; **Imagemore Co., Ltd:** 29tl (Guitar); **Pearson Education Ltd:** Studio 8 90cr/7, Trevor Clifford 50tl, 50tr, 50cl, 50cr, 51tr, 52t, 104cr, 104br, 105cr, 105br, Malcolm Harris 59bl (Rabbit), Tudor Photography 41tr (Boy); **PhotoDisc:** C Squared Studios / Tony Gable 28tc/b, Photolink 95c; **Shutterstock. com:** 3445128471 96bl, 15bl, 109bc (Boy), Hintau Aliaksei 109br (Frog), Petrenko Andriy 20b, Venus Angel 68tl/1, Apollofoto 47cr, Artcasta 86tc/4, Arvind Balaraman 110tr, Baloncici 68tc/3, Beata Becla 74tl/1, Bochkarev Photography 81c (Fish), Mark Bonham 55t, Ekaterina V. Borisova 109bc (Rabbit), Butterfly Hunter 18c (Butterfly), Kenneth William Caleno. 86c/8, Cheryl Casey 90tc/3, Massimo Cattaneo 62tl/1, Jacek Chabraszewski 52br, 110cl, Steven Chiang 28bl, Lucian Coman 94c/2, 94bc/c, Corepics VOF. 72br/c, Couperfield 84bc/3, Cre8tive Images 80tl/4 (Chocolate), 80c (Chocolate), Creative_soul 40bc/2, CreativeNature.nl. 64c/e, Vladyslav Danilin 81cr (Cheese), Deklofenak 73c (Shop), DenisNata 96cl/a, Serg Dibrova 19tl (Fish), Elena Efimova 63cl, Elena Elisseeva 63cr, F9photos 110tc/a, Slawomir Fajer 90c/6, Fotomak 94tr, FrameAngel. 68c/6, Terri Francis 72tl, Filip Fuxa 72c, Gelpi JM 25cr, 51tl, 84tc, 96br, 102cl, Gengirl 63tc, Deyan Georgiev 96cr/d, Volodymyr Goinyk 94tc, Stephen B. Goodwin 109cr/d, 109bc (Snake), Joe Gough 80tr/3, 80c (Meat), 85cl (Meat), Hainaultphoto 95tl, Brent Hofacker 86cr/10, Jiang Hongyan 109br (Rabbit), Mau Horng 80c (Cake), 86cl/6, Hwongcc 18tr (Rose), Hxdbzxy 59bl (Hamster), Hyena Reality 73c (Park), Iofoto 107cr, Smolych Iryna 72cl, Eric Isselee 59bl (Puppy), 109bc (Spider), Italianestro 28tr/c, Jackhollingsworth.com 111cl/2, Matt Jeppson 64cr/c, JFunk 74br, Jirasaki 15br, 109bl (Girl), JStudio 37bl, Junial Enterprises 25cr, 102cr, Alex Kalashnikov 63c (Hamster), Kamira 59br, 84cr, Karamysh 74tr/5, Vladimir Koletic 29tc (Singer), Vasiliy Koval 109cr/c, Dmitriy Krasko 84br/4, Philip Lange 110c/d, Lana Langlois 64cr/f, Leungchopan 29tc (Violin), Stephen Lew 94cl/1, 94bc/b, Veronica Louro 110tl, Lubava 62c/b, Cosmin Manci 18cr (Butterfly), R. Gino Santa Maria 81tc, 91bc, 91br, Nataliia Melnychuk 64c/b, Mexrix 84bl/5, 85cl (Yogurt), 86c/7, Michelle D. Milliman 29tr (Violinist), MishAl 68tr/4, Monkey Business Images 109tc, Mylisa 80c (Cheese), 84bc/2, Olga Nayashkova 86tr/5, Nbriam 18c (Leaf), Neamov 28tc/d, Nejron Photo 42c (c), Newphotoservice 72tc, Tomasz Niewęglowski 40bc/3, Nito 80tl/1, 80c (Jello), 81cl (Jello), Sergey Novikov 59bc, Odua Images 42cl (a), Outdoorsman 95tc, Paul Matthew Photography 111bl/4, Siamionau Pavel 84bl/1, Preto Perola 84bc/6, Phase4Studios 110cr, Photolinc 109br (Rat), Pr2is 94c/3, 94br/d, Inara Prusakova 40tl, Tatjana Rittner 18c (Fish), Room27 68cl/5, Rossario. 72br/d, Dario Sabljak 28tl/a, Pablo Scapinachis 74tc/2, SergiyN 31bl, 53b, Serp 18br (Maple leaf), Anastasia Shilova 64bl, Artazum and Iriana Shiyan 74tc/3, 74tc/4, Shyamalamuralinath 52bl, Sixninepixels 68c/7, Ljupco Smokovski 80tc/2, 80c (Honey), 81c (Honey), 85c (Honey), Solnechnaja 110c/c, Tracy Starr 59bl (Parrot), Stockyimages 95cr, Tatjana Strelkova 59bl (Kitten), Syda Productions 19tr, 90tr/4, TijanaM 64br, Tobyphotos 19tl (Butterfly), Tratong 109br (Iguana), Solomiya Trylovska 28br, TTstudio 18cl (Daffodil), Urfin 62tr/3, 62cl/a, Vishnevskiy Vasily 18tl (Bird), Wavebreakmedia 28cl, 86b, Wckiw 51tc (Boy), Tony Wear 109br (Mouse), Monika Wisniewska 42cr (d), Anke van Wyk 62tc/2, Wong Sze Yuen 73cr, Zurbagan. 86tl/1; **SuperStock:** Ingram Publishing / Alamy 96c/c

All other images © Pearson Education

Every effort has been made to trace the copyright holders and we apologize in advance for any unintentional omissions. We would be pleased to insert the appropriate acknowledgement in any subsequent edition of this publication.

Contents

Scope and sequence

Welcome

Vocabulary:	Colors: blue, green, red, yellow
	Numbers: zero, one, two, three, four, five, six, seven, eight, nine, ten
Structures:	Hello. I'm Mandy.
	Goodbye.

1 My birthday

Vocabulary:	Colors: pink, purple, orange, brown, black, white, gray	Values: It's good to share.
	Numbers: eleven, twelve, thirteen, fourteen, fifteen	Cross-curricular: Science: Nature
Structures:	What's your name? My name's Cody. How old are you? I'm seven.	Phonics: a, p, s, t
	Is it purple? Yes, it is. / No, it isn't.	at, pat, sat, tap
	What color is it? It's pink.	

2 At school

Vocabulary:	Classroom objects: pencil case, pencil, pencil sharpener, ruler, eraser, pen, book	Values: Try hard at school.
	More classroom words: backpack, table, chair, board, desk, classroom, school, student	Cross-curricular: Music: Musical instruments
Structures:	What's this? It's a book. It's red. It's a red book.	Phonics: d, i, m, n
	Are they blue? Yes, they are. / No, they aren't.	dad, it, am, nap
	What color are they? They're white.	

3 My family

Vocabulary:	Family members: sister, brother, friend, aunt, mom, dad, grandmother, grandfather	Values: Love your family.
	Occupations: a vet, a pilot, a doctor, a teacher, a cook, a farmer, a dentist, an artist	Cross-curricular: Art: Types of art
		Phonics: c, g, o
Structures:	This is my brother/sister.	cat, gas, on
	How old is he/she? He's/She's nine.	
	Is he/she a vet/an artist?	
	Yes, he/she is. / No, he/she isn't. He's/She's a cook.	

4 My body

Vocabulary:	Parts of the body: arms, head, body, legs, hands, feet	Values: Be clean.
	More parts of the body: fingers, toes, shoulders, neck, knee, elbow	Cross-curricular: Social science: Personal hygiene
Structures:	I have a green tail.	Phonics: ck, e, k
	I have green arms.	sock, pen, kit
	I have a head. It's yellow.	
	I have three arms. They're red.	

⑤ Pets

Vocabulary:	**Pets:** hamster, dog, cat, mouse, rabbit, parrot, snake, turtle, frog **Adjectives:** big, small, tall, short, long, young, old
Structures:	I have a dog. He/She has a dog. Do you have a parrot? Yes, I do. / No, I don't. Does he/she have a parrot? Yes, he/she does. No, he/she doesn't. He/She has a big dog.

Values: Take care of your pets.

Cross-curricular:
 Science: Baby animals

Phonics: b, h, r, u
 bag, hot, red, up

⑥ My house

Vocabulary:	**Places and things at home:** bedroom, living room, door, dining room, house, kitchen, bathroom, window **Household objects:** bed, stove, refrigerator, TV, sofa, lamp, tub, sink
Structures:	Where's Aunt Fifi? She's in the living room. Where are Waldo and Beth? They're in the bedroom. There's a lamp on the desk. There are two kittens under the sofa.

Values: Be neat.

Cross-curricular:
 Social science: Places in the neighborhood

Phonics: f, ff, l, ll
 fan, off, leg, doll

⑦ Food

Vocabulary:	**Food items:** fruit, salad, cake, bread, yogurt, milk, cheese, fish **More food items:** jello, honey, meat, chocolate, ice cream, juice
Structures:	I like cake and milk. I don't like salad and fish. Do you like honey? Yes, I do. / No, I don't.

Values: Be polite.

Cross-curricular:
 Food science: Healthy food

Phonics: j, ss, v, w
 jam, mess, vet, web

⑧ I'm happy!

Vocabulary:	**Adjectives:** tired, hungry, thirsty, scared, happy **More adjectives:** sad, cold, hot, sick, hurt, angry, bored
Structures:	I'm hungry. He's/She's thirsty. Are you happy? Yes, I am. / No, I'm not. Is he/she happy? Yes, he/she is. / No, he/she isn't.

Values: Respect feelings. Help others.

Cross-curricular:
 Geography: Hot and cold places

Phonics: qu, x, y, z, zz
 queen, box, yes, zip, buzz

Alphabet

1  **Listen, point, and say.**

ant

balloon

car

dinosaur

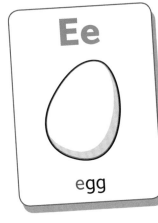
egg

feather

girl

helicopter

igloo

jam

key

lemon

map

noodles

Can pronounce the sound of each letter of the alphabet

octopus

pirate

queen

robot

sun

tiger

umbrella

vet

window

ox

yo-yo

zebra

2  A:03 / A:04 **Sing the alphabet song.**

A, B, C,
D, E, F,
G, H, I, J,
K, L, M,
N, O, P,
Q, R, S,
T, U, V, W,
X, Y, and Z

Now I know my ABCs!
It's so easy!
Sing with me!
It's so easy!
Sing with me!

Welcome

1 A:05 **Listen and write. Then say.**

Harry   Beth   Waldo

2 A:06 **Listen and find.**

Beth.   Blue.

a blue   b green   c red   d yellow

3 Point and say.

Can identify colors

4 **A:07 / A:08** **Listen and chant.**

See the colors of the flowers.
Red, red flowers. Yellow, yellow flowers.
Colors, colors, everywhere.
Blue, blue flowers. Green, green flowers.
Colors, colors, everywhere.

Cody   Aunt Fifi

5 **A:09** **Listen and circle. Then say.**

A red flower.

1   a   b
2   a   b
3   a   b
4   a   b

6  **Listen and say.**

0 1 2 3 4 5

zero   one   two   three   four   five

6   7   8   9   10

six   seven   eight   nine   ten

7 **Listen and chant.**

one   two   three   four   five

six   seven   eight   nine   ten

Now count again!

8   **Count and write.**

①

②

③

9 **Listen and circle.**

1 (Hello. / Goodbye.)

2 (Hello. / Goodbye.)

10  **Listen and sing.**

 **SONG**

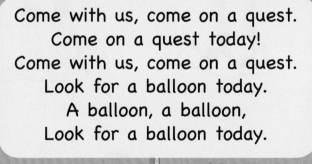

Come with us, come on a quest.
Come on a quest today!
Come with us, come on a quest.
Look for a balloon today.
A balloon, a balloon,
Look for a balloon today.

1 My birthday

1 ⭐ **What do you know?**

pink

purple

orange

brown

2 🎧 A:15 **Listen.**

3 🎧 A:16 **Listen and number.**

4 🎧 A:17 **Listen and say.**

Can identify more colors

5  **Listen and chant.**

Name, name. What's your name?
Beth, Beth. My name's Beth.

Age, age. How old are you?
Six, six. I'm six.

black

white

gray

LOOK!

What's your name?	My name's Cody.
How old are you?	I'm seven.

What's = What is

6 **Listen and write. Then ask and answer.**

What's your name?

My name's Waldo.

How old are you?

I'm _____!

Quest

7  **Listen and say.**

11
eleven

12
twelve

13
thirteen

14
fourteen

15
fifteen

8  **Look at Activity 7. Listen and circle.**

9 **Listen and circle. Then sing and act.**

Happy Birthday!

It's my birthday!
Hip hip hooray! Happy Birthday!
Clap, clap, clap!
I'm (7 / 11) today!

It's my birthday!
Hip hip hooray! Happy Birthday!
Stamp, stamp, stamp!
I'm (14 / 12) today!

It's my birthday!
Hip hip hooray! Happy Birthday!
Jump, jump, jump!
I'm (13 / 11) today!
Happy birthday! Happy birthday!

10 Listen and stick.

LOOK!

Is it purple?	Yes, **it is.** / No, **it isn't.**
What color is it?	**It's** pink.

isn't = is not   It's = It is

 1

2

 3

4

Stick

 11 Look and play.

SPEAKING

1

2

3

4

Is it pink?

Number 3!

Yes, it is.

Lesson 4

Can ask and answer about colors using *What color is it?*

15

1

13   **Role-play the story.**

14 **Read the story again. Match and color.**

1 Beth

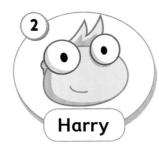
2 Harry

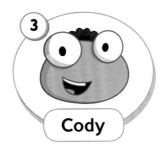
3 Cody

4 Waldo

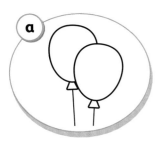
a

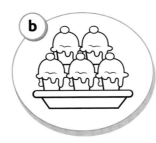
b

c

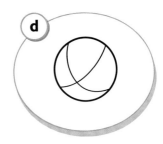
d

VALUES

It's good to share.

15 **Look and stick.**

Stick

16 Listen and point. Then say.

1
bird

2
fish

3
flower

4
leaf

5
butterfly

17  Complete the pictures. Then say.

1

2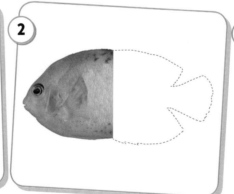

3

4

5

18 Make a poster about animals and plants.

Animals and plants

Animals

Plants

A red flower.

HOME SCHOOL LINK

Show your poster to your family.

19  A:31 Listen.

① **at**   ② **pat**   ③ **sat**   ④ **tap**

20  A:32 Listen and blend the sounds.

21 Underline *a*, *p*, and *t*. Read the words aloud.

1   pat

2   tap

22 ✏ **Write and color.**

1 pink

2 brown

3 purple

4 white

5 black

6 orange

7 gray

23 🎧 A:33 **Listen and check (✓). Then say.**

1
a
b

2
a
b

3
a
b

4
a
b

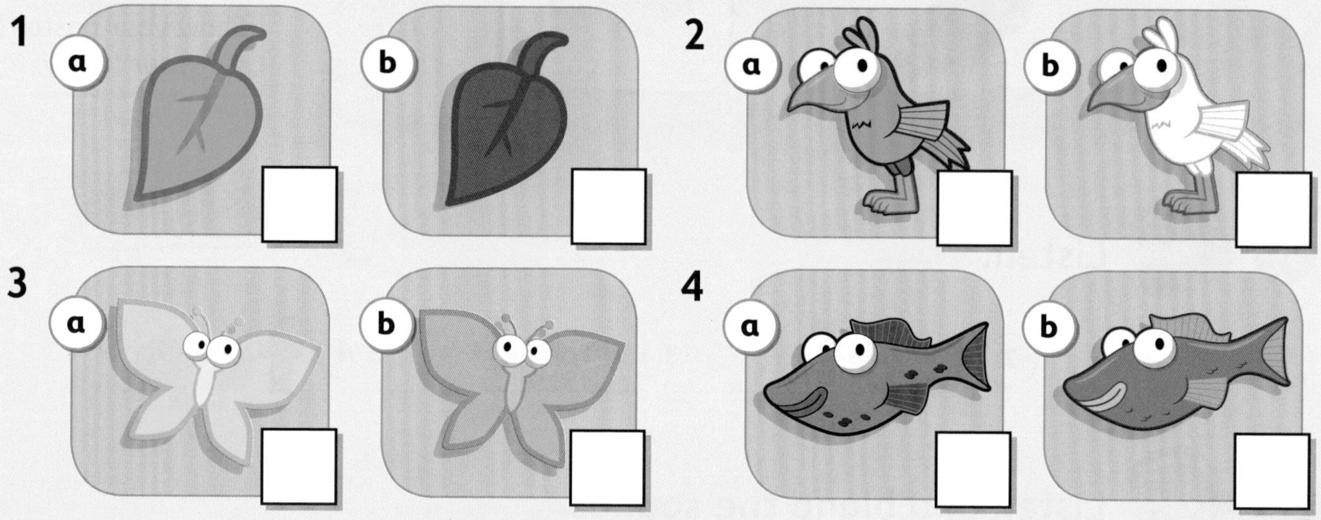

24 **Write. Then ask and answer.**

What's your name?

How old are you?

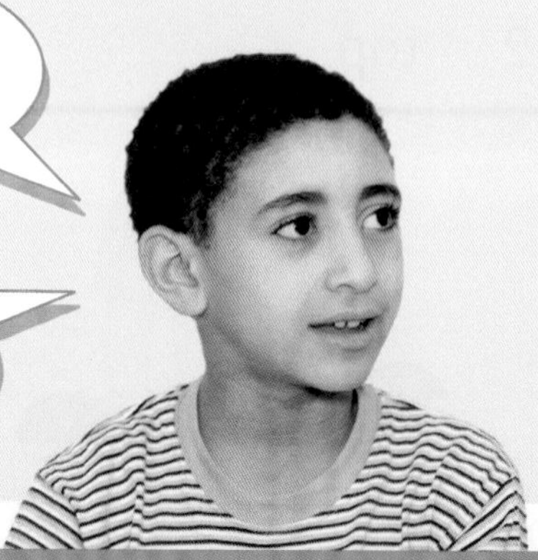

My name's _____.

I'm _____.

Can assess what I have learned in Unit 1

25 Find, count, and write.

1	2	3	4	5	6

26  Find and say.

Three red balloons.

Now go to Poptropica English World

Lesson 10 Can use what I have learned in Unit 1 **21**

2 At school

1 ⭐ What do you know?

pencil case

pencil

pencil sharpener

ruler

2  Listen.

3  Listen and circle.

4 Listen and say.

Can identify classroom objects

5 A:37 / A:38 **Listen and chant.**

A yellow pencil and a blue pen.
A pink pencil case and an orange pencil sharpener.
A green ruler and a white eraser.
A purple book. Look, look, look!

book

eraser

pen

TIP!
It's a book.
It's an eraser.

A:39 **LOOK!**

What's this?
It's a book. It's red.
It's a red book.

6 A:40 **Listen and number. Then ask and answer.**

a

b

c

d

What's this?

It's a yellow pen.

Quest
A:41

7 **Listen and say.**

a

backpack

b

table

c

chair

d

board

e

desk

f

classroom

g

school

h

student

TIP!

one desk
two desks

8 **Listen, count, and circle the numbers.**
   Then sing and act.

SONG

Backpacks, backpacks,
(Two / Four) red backpacks.
They are red. Red, red, red!
Hooray! Let's play! Let's jump and climb!

Books, books,
(Five / Seven) blue books.
They are blue. Blue, blue, blue!
Hooray! Let's play!
Let's jump and climb!

Tables, tables,
(Three / Six) brown tables.
They are brown.
Brown, brown, brown!
Hooray! Let's play!
Let's jump and climb!

Can identify more classroom objects

9 Listen and circle. Then ask and answer.

LOOK!

Are they blue?	Yes, **they are**.
	No, **they aren't**.
What color are they?	**They're** white.

aren't = are not   They're = They are

1 a    b

2 a    b

3 a    b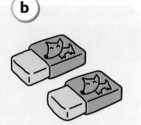

4 a    b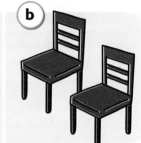

 What color are they?

 They're blue.

10 Listen and stick.

LISTENING

1 [ ]   2 [ ]   3 [ ]   4 [ ]

Stick

12   **Role-play the story.**

13 **Read the story again. Find and check (✓).**

1

a

b

2

a

b

3

a

b

4

a

b

14 **Look and stick.**

✓

Do at school.

✗

Don't do at school.

Stick

15 A:49 **Listen and number. Then say.**

a

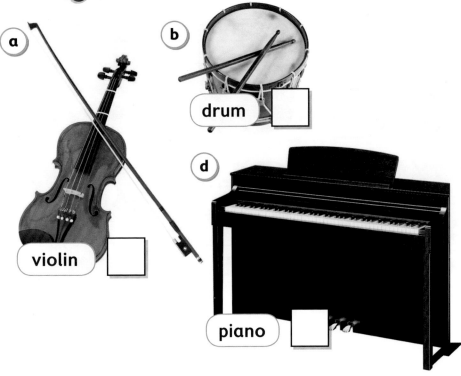

b

drum ☐

d

c

violin ☐

piano ☐

guitar ☐

16 A:50 **Listen and number.**

 ☐

 ☐

 ☐

 ☐

17 Make a poster about musical instruments.

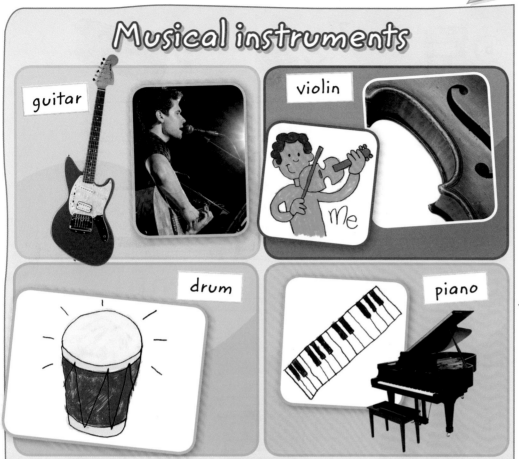

Musical instruments

guitar

violin

drum

piano

It's a violin.
It's blue.

HOME SCHOOL LINK

Show your poster to your family.

18 Listen.
A:51

1 dad   **2** it   **3** am   **4** nap

19 Listen and blend the sounds.
A:52

20 Underline *d, i, m,* and *n*. Then read the words aloud.

1 man   **2** dip   **3** nap   **4** pan   **5** sit   **6** dad

21 **Write and circle.**

1

a    b

<u>desk</u>

2

a    b

<u>pencil case</u>

3

a    b

<u>classroom</u>

4

a    b

<u>student</u>

22 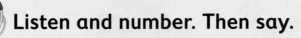 **Listen and number. Then say.**

A:53

a  ☐   b  ☐   c  ☐   d  ☐

23 **Color. Then ask and answer.**

1    **2**

It's a red guitar.

What's this?

3    **4**

Can assess what I have learned in Unit 2

24 **Find and circle six differences.**

1

2

25 **Say and play.**

A pink pencil case.

Picture 1.

Now go to Poptropica English World

 **1** Write and color. Then say.

 1   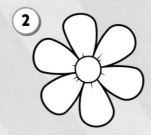 2    3    4

It's __blue__.   It's __orange__.   It's __purple__.   It's __brown__.

 2 Listen and write.

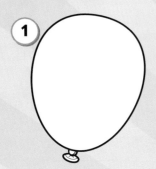 1   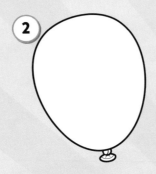 2   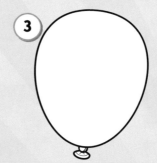 3    4

 3 Count and write. Then say.

 1   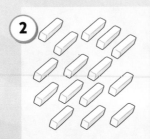 2   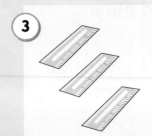 3    4

_____   _____   _____   _____

4  **Listen and check (✓).**

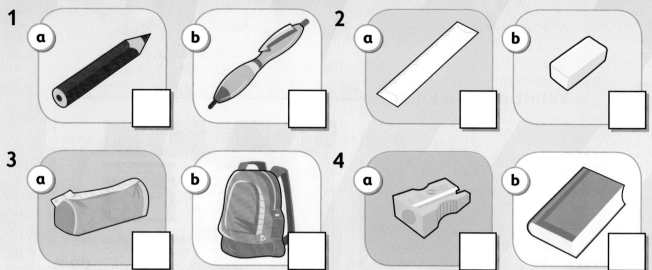

1 a (pencil) ☐   b (pen) ☐

2 a (ruler) ☐   b (eraser) ☐

3 a (pencil case) ☐   b (backpack) ☐

4 a (sharpener) ☐   b (book) ☐

5  **Draw. Then write and circle.**

It's a (<u>table / chair</u>).

6  **Listen and number.**

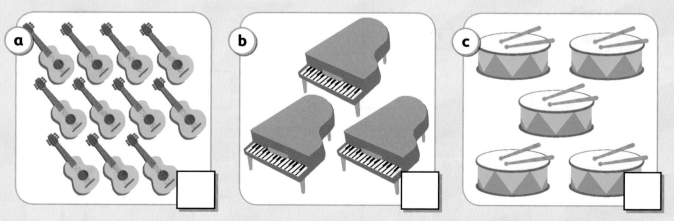

a ☐   b ☐   c ☐

3 My family

1 ⭐ **What do you know?**

sister

brother

friend

aunt

2 🎧 A:57 **Listen.**

3 🎧 A:58 **Listen and number.**

4 🎧 A:59 **Listen and say.**

 a

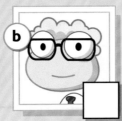 b

 c

 d

 e

 f

 g

 h

Can identify family members

5  Listen and chant.

This is my sister.
How old is she?
She's six, she's six!

This is my brother.
How old is he?
He's seven, he's seven!

 mom

 dad

 grandmother

 grandfather

LOOK!

A:62

This is	my brother/sister.
How old is he/she?	**He's/She's** nine.

He's = He is   She's = She is

6  Listen and write. Then ask and answer.

1  10

2

3

4

How old is he?

He's ten.

Quest A:64

7 🎧 A:65 **Listen and point.**

a **a vet** ☐

b **a pilot** ☐

c **a doctor** ☐

d **a teacher** ☐

e **a cook** ☐

f **a farmer** ☐

g **a dentist** ☐

h **an artist** ☐

8 🎧 A:66 **Look at Activity 7. Listen and number. Then say.**

9 🎧 A:67 / A:68 **Listen and match. Then sing and act.**

SONG

I'm at the airport with my family.
Brother, sister, mom, and dad.
I'm glad, glad, glad!

This is my mom. She's a pilot.
My dad is a pilot, too.
This is my sister. She's happy!
But my brother is sad.

I'm at the airport
With my family.
Brother, sister, mom, and dad.
I'm glad, glad, glad!
I'm glad, glad, glad!
I'm glad, glad, glad!
I'm glad, glad, glad!

my sister   my brother   my mom

me   my dad

Can identify occupations

LOOK!

A:69

Is he/she	a vet?	Yes, **he/she is.**
	an artist?	No, **he/she isn't.**
		He's/She's a cook.

Stick

10  A:70 **Listen and stick.**

| 1 | 2 | 3 | 4 |

11 **Look and play.** **SPEAKING**

 1
 2
 3
 4

 5
 6
 7
 8

Is she a pilot?

Number 1!

No, she isn't.
She's an artist.

Listen to the story. Read.

  Role-play the story.

Can understand a simple story / Can role-play a story

14 Read the story again. Look and check (✓).

1

a

b

2

a

b

3

a

b

 **15** Listen and stick.

I love my family.

①

②

③

④

 Stick

16 **Listen and number. Then say.**

a

painting

b

collage

c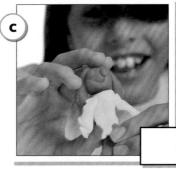

sculpture

d

drawing

 17 **Listen. Then ask and answer.**

1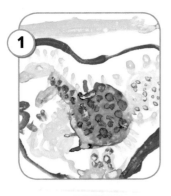

2

3

4

Is it a painting?

Yes, it is.

Is it a dragon?

Yes, it is.

Can identify different types of art

18 Make a poster about art.

It's a painting.

HOME SCHOOL LINK

Show your poster to your family.

19  Listen.

1 cat   **2** gas   **3** on

20 Listen and blend the sounds.

21  Underline *c*, *g*, and *o*. Then read the words aloud.

1 dig   **2** cap   **3** dog   **4** on   **5** gas   **6** can

22 Write and number.

1 dad   **2** aunt   **3** grandmother

4 grandfather   **5** mom   **6** friend

23 A:77 Listen and number. Then say.

a   b   c   d

24 Ask and answer.

Is he a sailor?

No, he isn't.

Is he a teacher?

Yes, he is.

ABC

25 Find and circle.

1
a  b

2
a  b

3
a  b

4
a  b

26 Say.

She's a doctor.

This is my mom.

Now go to Poptropica
English World

4 My body

1 ⭐ **What do you know?**

head

hands

body

arms

legs

feet

2 🎧 B:02 **Listen.**

3 🎧 B:03 **Listen and number.**

4 🎧 B:04 **Listen and say.**

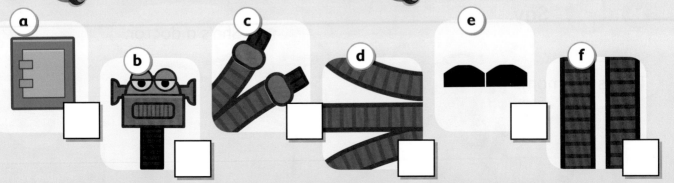

a

b

c

d

e

f

44 **Lesson 1**

Can identify parts of the body

5 B:05 / B:06 **Listen and chant.**

I have green arms.
I have green hands.
I have green legs.
I have green feet.
I have green wings.
I have a green tail.
I have a green head,
But now it's red!

TIP!
one foot
two feet

B:07 **LOOK!**

| I have | a green tail. |
| | green arms. |

6 B:08 **Listen and circle. Then say and play.**

1 2 3

I have black feet.

Number 2.

Quest B:09

7 B:10 **Listen and say. Then listen again and point.**

 a

fingers

b

toes

c

shoulders

d

neck

e

knee

f

elbow

8 B:11 / B:12 **Listen and circle the numbers. Then sing and act.**

 SONG

I have (2 / 3) hands.
Clap, clap, clap,
Clap your hands. (x2)

I have (4 / 2) feet.
Stamp, stamp, stamp,
Stamp your feet. (x2)

Clap, stamp, clap, stamp,
Clap your hands
And stamp your feet. (x2)

I have (5 / 8) fingers.
Snap, snap, snap,
Snap your fingers. (x2)

I have (8 / 6) toes.
Wiggle, wiggle, wiggle,
Wiggle your toes. (x2)

Snap, wiggle, snap, wiggle,
Snap your fingers
And wiggle your toes.(x2)

Can identify more parts of the body

9  **Listen and number.**
Then ask and answer.

B:13

LOOK!

I have a head. It's yellow.

three arms. They're red.

a

b

c

d

I have four arms. They're brown.

Number 1!

10  **Listen and stick. Then point and say.**

1

2

3

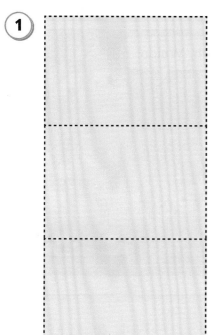

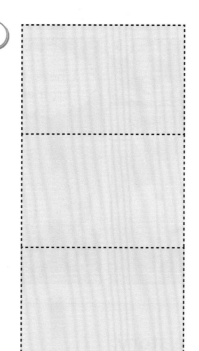

Stick

12   **Role-play the story.**

13 **Read the story again. Look and check (✓).**

1 a ☐   b ☐

2 a ☐   b ☐

3 a ☐   b ☐

14 **Stick. Then check (✓).**

VALUES
Be clean.

1 ☐   2 ☐   3 ☐

4 ☐   5 ☐   6 ☐

Stick

15   **Listen and number. Then say.**

a

clean hands ☐

b

dirty hands ☐

c

a dirty face ☐

d

Wash your hands! ☐

16 **Look and circle or write.**

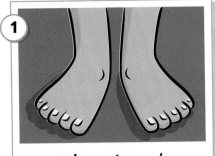

1

clean toes /
dirty toes

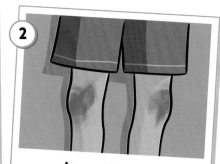

2

clean knees /
dirty knees

3

Wash your hands! /
Wash your face!

4

dirty neck

5

clean hands

Can understand clean and dirty, and instructions to wash parts of my body

17 Make a poster about being clean.

Be Clean

dirty

clean

Be clean!

HOME
SCHOOL
LINK

Show your poster to
your family.

18  B:18 Listen.

① **sock** ② **pen** ③ **kit**

19  B:19 Listen and blend the sounds.

20  Underline *ck*, *e*, and *k*. Then read the words aloud.

1 pen   **2** kid   **3** neck   **4** sock   **5** kick   **6** kit

21 ✎ **Write and draw lines.**

1 head
2 elbow
3 leg
4 shoulder
5 arm
6 knee
7 body

22 🎧 B:20 **Write. Then listen and ✓ or ✗.**

I have _____ feet.

1 ☐	2 ☐
3 ☐	4 ☐
5 ☐	6 ☐

23 **Look. Then ask and answer.**

I have three heads.

False.

I have a purple body.

True.

Can assess what I have learned in Unit 4

Find and circle two the same. Then say.

24

1

2

3

25 **Color. Then play.**

I have green legs.

I have four arms. They're orange.

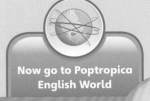

Now go to Poptropica English World

Review  Units 3 and 4

1 Listen and number.

 a

 b

 c

 d

 e

 f

2  Listen and write.

1   2   3

3 Listen and check (✓). Then ask and answer.

1  a    b

2  a    b

3  a    b

4 a    a    b

Can talk about family members and occupations

4 Look and write.

1 __head__

2 __arm__

3 __hand__

4 __body__

5 __leg__

6 __foot__

She's a __dancer__ .

5 Listen and draw.

B:24

1

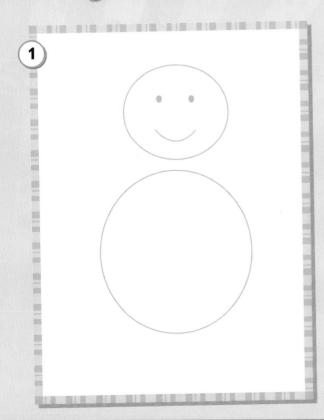

2

5 Pets

1 What do you know?

hamster

mouse

dog

cat

rabbit

5 **B:28 / B:29** **Listen and chant.**

Pets, pets. Big and small!
Come and listen to them all.

I have a parrot, a big parrot.
She has a mouse, a small mouse.
He has a rabbit, a big rabbit.

I have a frog, a small frog.
She has a cat, a big cat.
He has a dog, a small dog.

So many pets.
Big and small!

parrot

snake

turtle

frog

TIP!
one mouse
two mice

B:30 **LOOK!**

I have a dog. He/She has a dog.

6 **B:31** **Listen and match. Then say and play.**

1 2 3 4 5

a b c d e

Quest

B:32

He has a rabbit. Number 1.

7  Listen and say. Then listen again and number.

a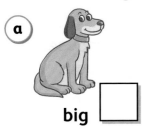
big ☐

b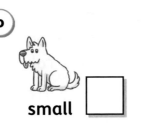
small ☐

c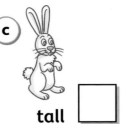
tall ☐

d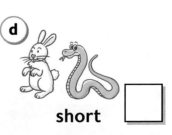
short ☐

e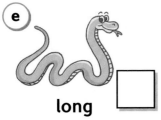
long ☐

f
young ☐

g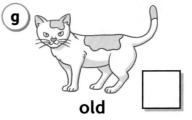
old ☐

8  Listen and circle. Then sing and act.

SONG

The boy has a dog

A very / .

He has a dog. Woof! Woof!

The dog has a frog

A very / .

The dog has a frog. Croak! Croak!

The girl has a cat

A very / .

She has a cat. Meow!

The cat has a hat

A very / .

The cat has a hat. Meow!

He has a dog.

The dog has a frog.

She has a cat,

And the cat has a hat!

Can recognize ways to describe pets

LOOK!

B:36

Do you	have a parrot?	Yes, I **do**.
		No, I **don't**.
Does he/she		Yes, he/she **does**.
		No, he/she **doesn't**. He/She **has** a big dog.

don't = do not   doesn't = does not

9 Listen and stick.
B:37

Stick

 1

 2

 3

 4

10 Listen. Then ask and answer.
B:38

SPEAKING

Find someone who...

has a cat.		
has a dog.		
has a rabbit.		
has a hamster.		
has a parrot.		

Maria has a cat. Alex has a dog.

Do you have a dog?

Yes, I do.

12 **Role-play the story.**

13 Read the story again. Look and number.

a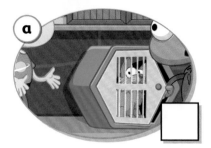

b

c

d

e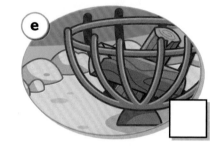

f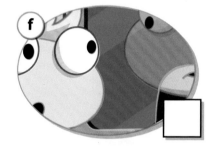

VALUES

Take care of your pets.

14 Look and stick.

1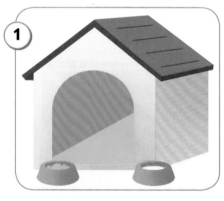

2

3

4

5

6

Stick

15 B:40 **Listen and point. Then match and say.**

1
cat

2
dog

3
bird

a
chick

b
kitten

c
puppy

16 B:41 **Listen and number. Then say.**

a
goose

b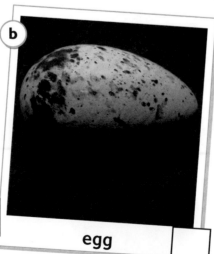
egg

c
chick

It's an egg.

Can identify baby animals

17 Make a poster about pets.

My Pets Poster

I have a puppy!

HOME SCHOOL LINK

Show your poster to your family.

18  Listen.

① **bag**   ② **hot**   ③ **red**   ④ **up**

19 Listen and blend the sounds.

20 Underline *b*, *h*, *r*, and *u*. Then read the words aloud.

1 rat   **2** cup   **3** tub   **4** hat   **5** red   **6** bag

Can make a poster about pets / Can use the sounds *b, h, r,* and *u*

21 Read and match.

1  2  3  4  5  6

a cat b parrot c rabbit d hamster e dog f turtle

  22 Listen and number. Then say.
B:44

a  b  c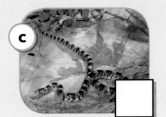

d 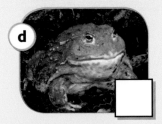 e  f

  23 Ask and answer.

Do you have a cat?

No, I don't.

Do you have a hamster?

Yes, I do.

Can assess what I have learned in Unit 5

24 **Play.**

25 **Listen and do.**

Now go to Poptropica
English World

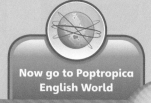

6 My house

1 ⭐ **What do you know?**

bedroom

house

door

2 🎧 **B:46** **Listen.**

living room

dining room

3 🎧 **B:47** **Listen and number.**

4 🎧 **B:48** **Listen and say.**

a

b

c

d

e

f

g

h

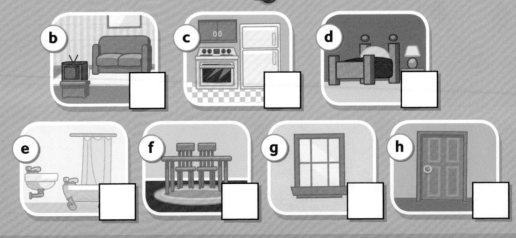

Can identify places and things at home

5 B:49 / B:50 **Listen and chant.**

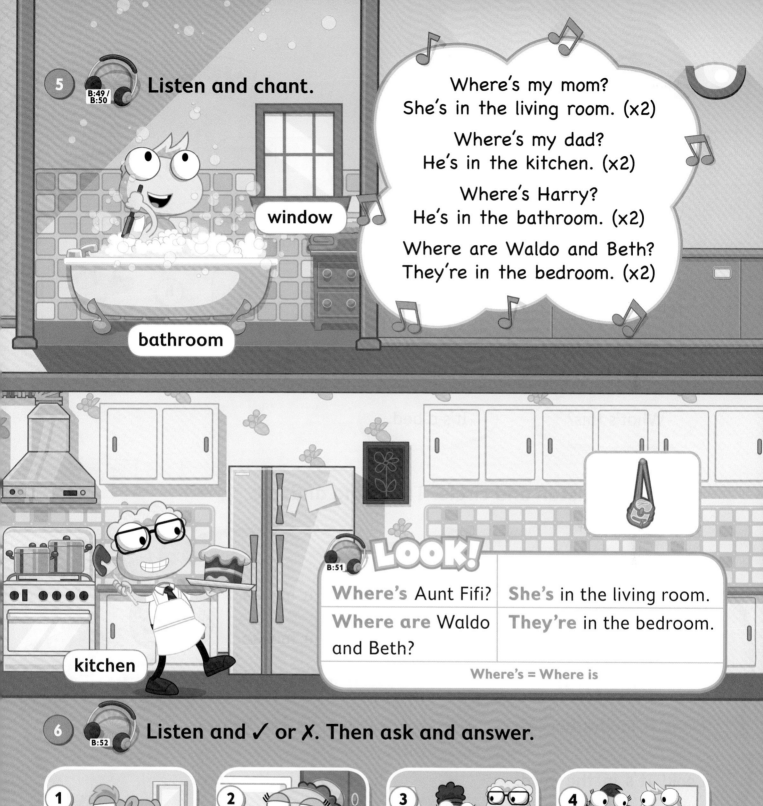

window

bathroom

♪ Where's my mom?
She's in the living room. (x2)

Where's my dad?
He's in the kitchen. (x2)

Where's Harry?
He's in the bathroom. (x2)

Where are Waldo and Beth?
They're in the bedroom. (x2) ♪

kitchen

B:51 **LOOK!**

Where's Aunt Fifi?	She's in the living room.
Where are Waldo and Beth?	They're in the bedroom.

Where's = Where is

6 B:52 **Listen and ✓ or ✗. Then ask and answer.**

Where's Waldo?   He's in the bathroom.

B:53

7   Listen and say. Then ask and answer.

a

bed

b

stove

c

refrigerator

d

TV

e

sofa

f

lamp

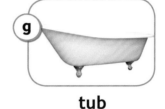
g

tub

h

sink

What's this?

It's a bed.

8   Listen and circle. Then sing and act.

SONG

There's a mouse.

There's a mouse.

Is it in the yard?

Or is it in the house?

Look! It's in the yard.

Running round a shrub.

Now it's in the / .

Oh, no! It's in the / !

There's a mouse.

There's a mouse.

Is it in the yard?

Or is it in the house?

Look! It's in the yard.

Hiding in the shed.

Now it's in the / .

Oh, no! It's in my /  !

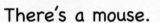

9 Listen and check (✓).

B:58

LOOK!

B:57

There's a lamp on the desk.

There are two kittens under the sofa.

There's = There is

6

1

a  b

2

a  b

3

a 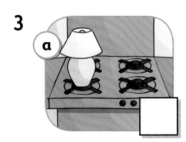 b

TIP!

under

on

in

10 Listen and stick. Then ask and answer.

B:59

LISTENING

1  2 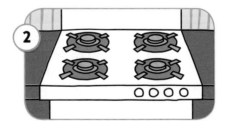 3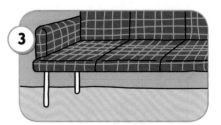

4  5  6

There are two books on the desk.

Number 6.

Stick

Listen to the story. Read.

12   **Role-play the story.**

Can understand a simple story / Can role-play a story

13 B:61 **Read the story again. Look and check (✓).**

1
(a)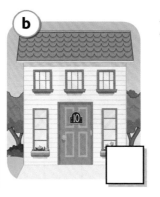
(b)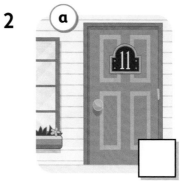

2
(a)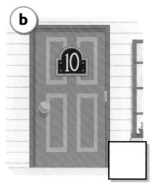
(b)

3
(a)
(b)

4
(a)
(b)

14 **Look and stick.**

VALUES

Be neat.

1
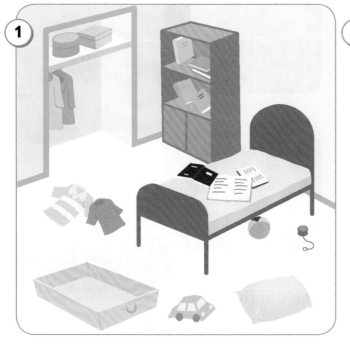

2

Stick

15 **Listen and number. Then say.**

SOCIAL SCIENCE

a

store ☐

b

library ☐

c

playground ☐

d

zoo ☐

e

yard ☐

 **16** **Listen and match. Then say.**

1

2

3

4

She's in the playground.

Can talk about places in the neighborhood

17 Make a poster about favorite places.

My Favorite Places

I'm in the library.

HOME SCHOOL LINK

Show your poster to your family.

18  B:64 Listen.

① **fan**   ② **off**   ③ **leg**   ④ **doll**

19  B:65 Listen and blend the sounds.

20  Underline *f*, *ff*, *l*, and *ll*. Then read the words aloud.

1 leg   **2** doll   **3** fig   **4** puff   **5** bell   **6** fan

21 **Look and write.**

1 _____ 2 _____ 3 _____ 4 _____ 5 _____
_____ _____ _____ _____ _____

22 **Look and check (✓). Then say.**

There's a sink in the kitchen.

23 **Ask and answer about your house.**

In my house, there are three bedrooms.

In my house, there's a TV in the kitchen.

74 **Lesson 9**   Can assess what I have learned in Unit 6

24 Find and circle. Then ask and answer.

LIBRARY

Corner MARKET

Where's Dad?

He's in the yard.

Now go to Poptropica English World

Lesson 10

Can use what I have learned in Unit 6

Review Units 5 and 6

1 Listen and ✓ or ✗.

 a

 b

 c

 d

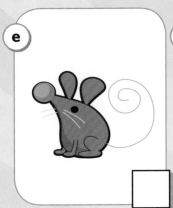 e

 f

 g

 h

2 Read and write.

dog rabbit snake turtle	big long small young

1 She has a

2 He has a

3 She has a

4 He has a

_____

_____ .

_____

_____ .

_____

_____ .

_____

_____ .

Can talk about pets

3 **Listen and match. Then ask and answer.**

1  **2**  **3**  **4**

a  **b**  **c**  **d**

 4 **Listen and draw.**

Can talk about places and things at home

7 Food

1 ⭐ **What do you know?**

fruit

salad

cake

bread

2 🎧 B:69 **Listen.**

3 🎧 B:70 **Listen and circle.**

4 🎧 B:71 **Listen and say.**

78 **Lesson 1**

Can identify food items

5 B:72 / B:73 **Listen and chant.**

> I like fruit and yogurt.
> I don't like fish and cheese.
> I like cake and milk and salad.
> Can I have some please?

yogurt

cheese

milk

fish

B:74 **LOOK!**

I **like** cake and milk.
I **don't like** salad and fish.

6 B:75 **Listen and match. Then ask and answer.**

I like fish.

You're Waldo.

Quest B:76

7 **B:77** Listen and point. Then listen again and ✓ or ✗. Then say.

① jello ☐

② honey ☐

③ meat ☐

④ chocolate ☐

⑤ ice cream ☐

⑥ juice ☐

8 **B:78 / B:79** Listen and circle. Then sing and act.

I like [jello] / [meat] . It's nice and sweet!

I like [ice cream] / [cake] . It's good to eat!

I like [juice] / [chocolate] . But I don't like [meat] / [cheese] .

I like [ice cream] / [honey] . But I don't like bees!

No, I don't like bees. (x3)

9 **Listen and stick. Then ask and answer.**

LOOK!

Do you like honey?	Yes, **I do.**
	No, **I don't.**

Stick

Do you like honey?

Yes, I do.

---

10 **Draw ☺ or ☹. Then ask and answer.**

SPEAKING

me	☺					
friend						

Do you like jello?

Yes, I do.

Listen to the story. Read.

  Role-play the story.

Can understand a simple story / Can role-play a story

13 B:83 **Listen and number.**

a

b

c

d

  14 B:84 **Listen and stick.**

 **VALUES**

Be polite.

1

2

3

4

 Stick

15   **Listen and number. Then say.**

a

b

c

16   **Check (✓) the foods that are healthy. Then say.**

I like salad. It's healthy.

I like chocolate, but it's unhealthy.

Can talk about healthy and unhealthy foods

17 Make a poster about healthy food.

I like fish. It's healthy.

HOME SCHOOL LINK

Show your poster to your family.

18 Listen. B:86 **PHONICS**

① **jam**   ② **mess**   ③ **vet**   ④ **web**

19 B:87 Listen and blend the sounds.

20 Underline *j*, *ss*, *v*, and *w*. Then read the words aloud.

1 jet   **2** wig   **3** kiss   **4** web   **5** van   **6** jam

21 **Look and write.**

 1
 2
 3
 4
 5

_____ _____ _____ _____ _____

 6
 7
 8
 9
 10

_____ _____ _____ _____ _____

22 **Draw and write. Then say.**

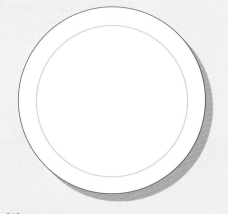

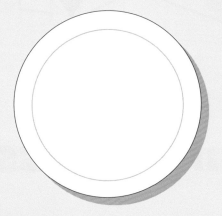

I like _____
and _____ .

I don't like _____
and _____ .

23 **Ask and answer.**

Do you like fish?

Yes, I do. It's healthy.

Can assess what I have learned in Unit 7

24 Find and draw ☺ or ☹. Then ask and answer.

I like chocolate.

You're Harry.

Now go to Poptropica
English World

Can use what I have learned in Unit 7

8 I'm happy!

1 ⭐ **What do you know?**

hungry

tired

thirsty

scared

happy

2  **Listen.**

3  **Listen and number.**

4 **Listen and say.**

 a

 b

 c

 d

 e

Lesson 1

Can identify feelings

5  **Listen and chant.**

> He's happy. Cody.
> She's thirsty. Beth.
> She's tired. Aunt Fifi.
> He's scared. Harry.
> He's hungry! Waldo.

Ice cream

JUICE

LOOK!

I'm hungry. | He's/She's thirsty.

6 **Listen and match. Then ask and answer.**

a   b   c   d   e

1   2   3   4   5

Waldo.

He's scared.

Quest

7   **Listen and say. Then ask and answer.**

1 sad

2 cold

3 hot

4 sick

He's hurt.

Number 5.

5 hurt

6 angry

7 bored

SONG

8  **Listen and circle. Then sing and act.**

5, 4, 3, 2, 1.
I'm (hot / cold)
And (sad / happy).
Let's have fun!

Clap your hands.
Stamp your feet.
Snap your fingers.
Drink and eat.

6, 7, 8, 9, 10.
I'm (hurt / cold)
And (sick / hot).
I'm going to bed!

Wiggle your toes.
Let's all lie down.
Roll over once.
Now turn around.

10, 8, 6, 4, 2.
I'm (angry / tired)
And (bored / scared).
Good night to you!

Can identify more feelings

9 **Look and circle.**

C:13 **LOOK!**

Are you happy?	Yes, **I am**.
	No, **I'm not**.
Is he/she happy?	Yes, **he/she is**.
	No, **he/she isn't**.

8

1

Is she happy?
(Yes, she is. /
No, she isn't.)

2

Is he angry?
(Yes, he is. /
No, he isn't.)

3

Are you happy?
(Yes, I am. /
No, I'm not.)

4

Are you cold?
(Yes, I am. /
No, I'm not.)

10  **Listen and stick. Then ask and answer.**
C:14

1  **2**  **3**  Stick

4

Is he angry?
Number 1.

Yes, he is.

Listen to the story. Read.

12 **Role-play the story.**

13 **Look and circle. Then listen and point.**

1. He's (sad / **angry**).

2. She's (cold / tired).

3. He's (sick / thirsty).

4. She's (happy / bored).

VALUES

Respect feelings. Help others.

14 **Read and stick.**

1. Are you sad?

2. Are you hurt?

3. Can I help you?

15 **Listen and say. Then circle.**

hot cold

1

2

3

It's (hot / cold).

It's (hot / cold).

It's (hot / cold).

16  **Listen and match. Then say.**

1

penguin

2

snake

3

polar bear

4

turtle

a

b

c

d

It's a snake.

It's hot.

17 Make a poster about animals in hot and cold places.

Animals in *hot* and *cold* places

hot	cold

It's hot!

HOME SCHOOL LINK

Show your poster to your family.

18  C:19 Listen.

① **queen** **②** **box** **③** **yes** **④** **zip** **⑤** **buzz**

19  C:20 Listen and blend the sounds.

20 Underline *qu, x, y, z,* and *zz.* Then read the words aloud.

1 zip   **2** taxi   **3** buzz   **4** yes   **5** quiz   **6** box

21 ✏️ **Look and write.**

1. I'm _____.
2. I'm _____.
3. I'm _____.
4. I'm _____.

22 🎧 C:21 **Listen and number. Then write.**

a) He's _____.

b) She's _____.

c) She's _____.

d) He's _____.

23 💬 **Ask and answer.**

Are you happy?

Yes, I am.

Are you sick?

No, I'm not.

Can assess what I have learned in Unit 8

24 **Find and match. Then ask and answer.**

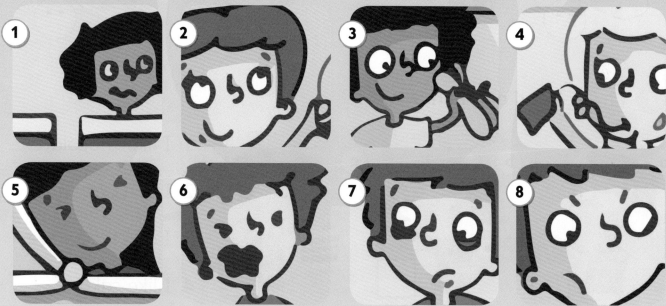

Is he scared?

Yes, he is.

Number 1.

Now go to Poptropica
English World

Lesson 10

Can use what I have learned in Unit 8

97

Review Units 7 and 8

 1 **C:22** Listen and draw.

Max

Anna

 2 Read and number.

a    **b**    **c**

1 I like chocolate.

2 I don't like honey.

3 I don't like juice.

4 I like cake.

d    **e**    **f**

5 I like ice cream.

6 I don't like jello.

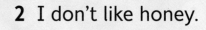

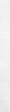

Can talk about food likes and dislikes

3 Listen and check (✓).

1

ⓐ   ☐   ⓑ   ☐

2

ⓐ   ☐   ⓑ   ☐

3

ⓐ   ☐   ⓑ   ☐

4

ⓐ   ☐   ⓑ   ☐

 4 Look and write.

1 She's

_____.

2 He's

_____.

3 She's

_____.

4 He's

_____.

Goodbye

1 C:24 Listen, find, and circle.

2 C:25 Listen and number.

a ⬜

b ⬜

c ⬜

d ⬜

e ⬜

f ⬜

g ⬜

h ⬜

i ⬜

Can identify the Quest items

3 Count and write. Then ask and answer.

There are ☐ Quest items.

a _____   b _____   c _____

d _____   e _____   f _____

g _____   h _____   i _____

There's a bird.   Yes!

4 **Look and find six differences. Say.**

1

2

In picture 1, he's happy.

In picture 2, he's sad.

 **5** **Listen and say. Then read and match.**

1 In picture 1,

2 In picture 1,

3 In picture 1,

4 In picture 2,

5 In picture 2,

6 In picture 2,

a he has a big dog.

b there are eight cakes.

c she has a blue book.

d there's a frog on the chair.

e he's happy.

f the mouse is on the chair.

Can use what I have learned

6  **Listen and sing.**

Come with us, come on a quest.
Come on a quest today!
Come with us, come on a quest.
Come on a quest today!

A balloon, a cake, a tablet, a photo,
A teddy bear, a bird, a door,
An apple and a hat...
We have them all today.

Goodbye! (x6)

7 **Draw and color. Then write.**

C:28

Food	School	Pet
_____	_____	_____

8 **Show a friend. Ask and answer.**

Is it a parrot?   Yes, it is.

Halloween

1 **Listen, find, and say.**

monster

witch

cat

pumpkin

bat

2  **Listen and chant.**

3  **Make and play.**

It's Halloween. It's Halloween.
Pass the pumpkin, 1, 2, 3.
Pass the pumpkin to me!

I'm a monster.
I'm a bat.
I'm a pumpkin.
I'm a witch. Ha, ha, ha!
And I have a cat.

It's Halloween. It's Halloween.
Pass the pumpkin, 1, 2, 3.
Pass the pumpkin to me!

Can chant a Halloween song and play a game

Christmas

1 C:32 Listen, find, and say.

Santa

present

reindeer

sleigh

2  C:33 / C:34 Listen and sing.

It's Christmas Day. It's Christmas Day.
Here comes Santa in his sleigh!
It's Christmas Day, it's Christmas Day.
Santa's on his way!

Look at the reindeer, 1, 2, 3.
Look at the presents! Can you see?
Red, yellow, green, and blue,
Orange, pink, and purple, too!

It's Christmas Day. It's Christmas Day.
Here comes Santa in his sleigh!
It's Christmas Day. It's Christmas Day.
Santa's on his way!
Merry Christmas!

3  Make and say.

Merry Christmas!

Mother's Day

1 **C:35** Listen, find, and say.

picnic

a card

flowers

HAPPY MOTHER'S DAY

HAPPY MOTHERS DAY

2 **C:36 / C:37** Listen and chant.

3 Make and say.

It's Mother's Day. It's Mother's Day.
A special day for Mom.
We make her cards, we give her flowers,
We spoil her all day long!

Happy Mother's Day! Happy Mother's Day!
It's time to thank you, Mom.
For all you do for me at home,
You spoil me all day long!

HAPPY MOTHER'S DAY, MOM!

Happy Mother's Day!

HAPPY Mother's Day

Can chant a song about Mother's Day

Father's Day

1 **C:38** Listen, find, and say.

a card

breakfast

slippers

newspaper

2  **C:39 / C:40** Listen and sing.

3 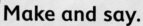 Make and say.

Happy Father's Day!

The children say,

It's Father's Day today!

Happy Father's Day!

Happy Father's Day!

It's Father's Day today! (x2)

HAPPY FATHER'S DAY, DAD!

Wider World 1

Carnivals around the world

1 **Read and match.**

1 It's Carnival time! There is carnival music. Look at the steel drums. How many drums can you see? What color are they?

2 This is a carnival float. It's a dragon. It's red and green. It has a red mouth and big teeth.

3 Carnival time is fun. I'm at the carnival with my sisters. We have blue and yellow costumes. We have masks, too.

a

b

c

2 **Make a carnival mask.**

Draw.

Cut.

Color and stick.

Play.

Can understand descriptions of carnivals around the world

Wider World 2

Unusual pets

1 **Read and circle. Then match.**

1  My name's Angela. I have a small pet. It's white, and it has four legs. It has a long tail. It's a (spider / rat).

2  My name's Ben. My pet is small and green. It has four legs and a tail. It's a (lizard / snake).

a  spider

b  lizard

3  My name's Grace. I have a small pet. It's brown and black, and it has eight legs. It's a (spider / lizard).

4 My name's Matt. My pet is long. It's brown. It doesn't have any legs! It's a (rat / snake).

c  rat

d  snake

2  **Ask and answer. Look and ✓ or ✗.**

Do you have a spider?

No, I don't.

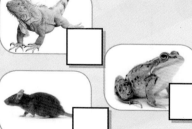

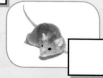

Wider World 3

Different homes

1   **Read and match.**

1  My name's Ella. I live in a small house. There's a kitchen, a living room, a bathroom, and three bedrooms. I have a big yard.

a

2  My name's Ravi. I live on a houseboat. It's a big boat. There's a kitchen, a bathroom, and two bedrooms. My favorite room is the kitchen.

b

3  My name's Rosie. I live in a mobile home! It's small, but it's nice. There's a living room, a kitchen, a bathroom, and two bedrooms.

c

4  My name's Juan. I live in a big apartment. There's a kitchen, a living room, two bathrooms, and four bedrooms. I have a TV in my bedroom.

d

2   **Ask and answer.**

Where do you live?

I live in an apartment.

What's your favorite room?

My favorite room is my bedroom.

Do you have a TV in your bedroom?

No, I don't.

Can talk about different homes and household objects

Wider World 4

Lunchboxes

1   **Read and match.**

1 I have sandwiches and fruit. I have a yogurt. I like milk, but I don't like juice.

2 I have bread and cheese and salad. I like salad, but I don't like fruit. I have chocolate and a juice.

3 I have sushi! It's fish and rice. I have fruit, and I have a cake. I don't like juice. I have water to drink.

4 I have chicken and salad. I don't like bread. I like juice, and I like chocolate. I don't like milk, and I don't like yogurt.

a

b

c

d

2 **Ask and answer.**

Do you like sandwiches?

Do you have a lunchbox?

What do you like for lunch?

Picture dictionary

Numbers

 zero

 one

two

three

 four

 five

 six

 seven

 eight

 nine

ten

eleven

 twelve

 thirteen

 fourteen

 fifteen

Colors

 red

 yellow

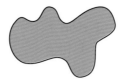 green

 blue

 gray

 pink

 purple

 orange

 brown

 black

 white

a

angry
p. 90

arms
p. 44

artist
p. 36

aunt
p. 34

b

backpack
p. 24

bathroom
p. 66

bed
p. 68

bedroom
p. 66

big
p. 58

board
p. 24

body
p. 44

book
p. 22

bored
p. 90

bread
p. 78

brother
p. 34

c

cake
p. 78

cat
p. 56

chair
p. 24

cheese
p. 78

chocolate
p. 80

classroom
p. 24

cold
p. 90

cook
p. 36

d

dad
p. 34

dentist
p. 36

desk
p. 24

dining room
p. 66

doctor
p. 36

dog
p. 56

door
p. 66

e

elbow
p. 46

eraser
p. 22

f

farmer
p. 36

feet
p. 44

fingers
p. 46

fish
p. 78

friend
p. 34

frog
p. 56

fruit
p. 78

g

grandfather ....
p. 34

grandmother ....
p. 34

h

hamster ....
p. 56

hands ....
p. 44

happy ....
p. 88

head ....
p. 44

honey ....
p. 80

hot ....
p. 90

house ....
p. 66

hungry ....
p. 88

hurt ....
p. 90

i

ice cream ....
p. 80

j

jello ....
p. 80

juice ....
p. 80

k

kitchen ....
p. 66

knee ....
p. 46

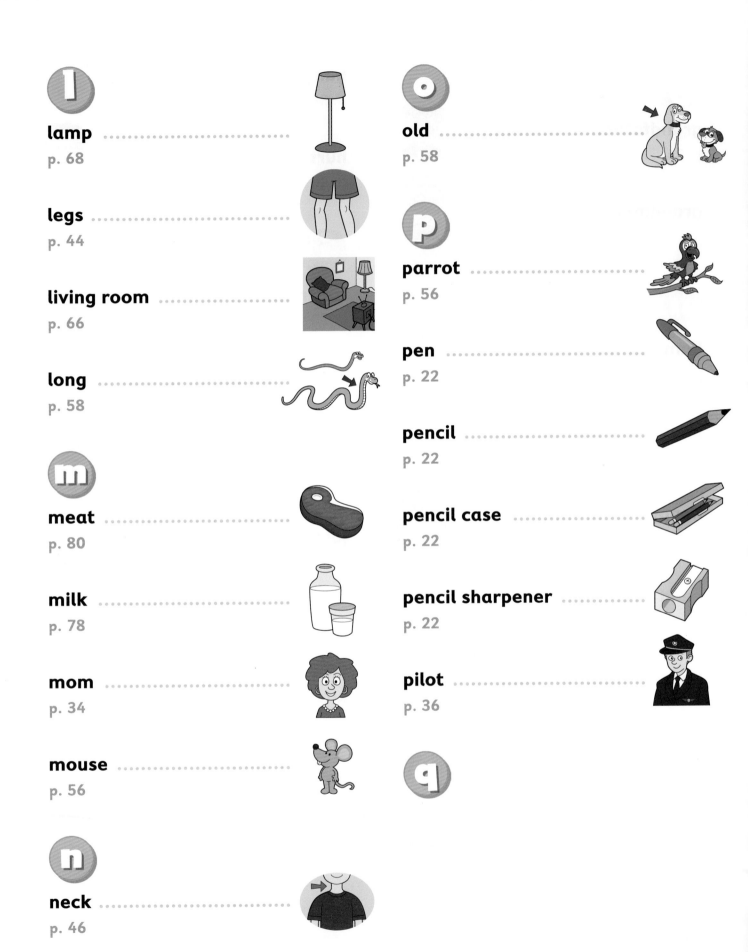

l

lamp
p. 68

legs
p. 44

living room
p. 66

long
p. 58

m

meat
p. 80

milk
p. 78

mom
p. 34

mouse
p. 56

n

neck
p. 46

o

old
p. 58

p

parrot
p. 56

pen
p. 22

pencil
p. 22

pencil case
p. 22

pencil sharpener
p. 22

pilot
p. 36

q

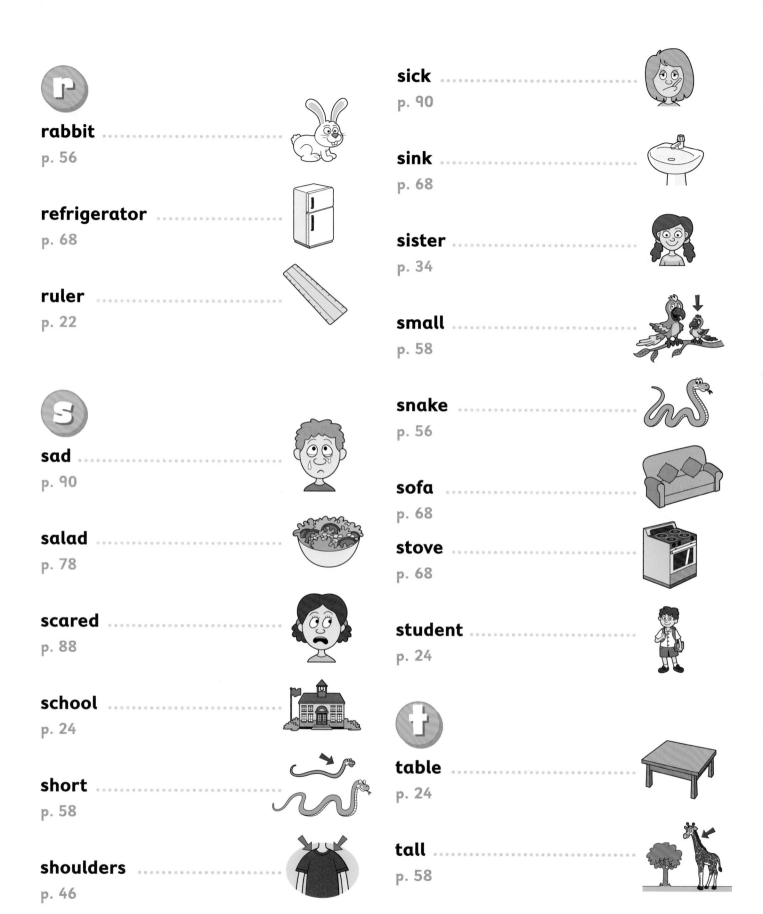

r

rabbit
p. 56

refrigerator
p. 68

ruler
p. 22

s

sad
p. 90

salad
p. 78

scared
p. 88

school
p. 24

short
p. 58

shoulders
p. 46

sick
p. 90

sink
p. 68

sister
p. 34

small
p. 58

snake
p. 56

sofa
p. 68

stove
p. 68

student
p. 24

t

table
p. 24

tall
p. 58

teacher
p. 36

thirsty
p. 88

tired
p. 88

toes
p. 46

tub
p. 68

turtle
p. 56

TV
p. 68

vet
p. 36

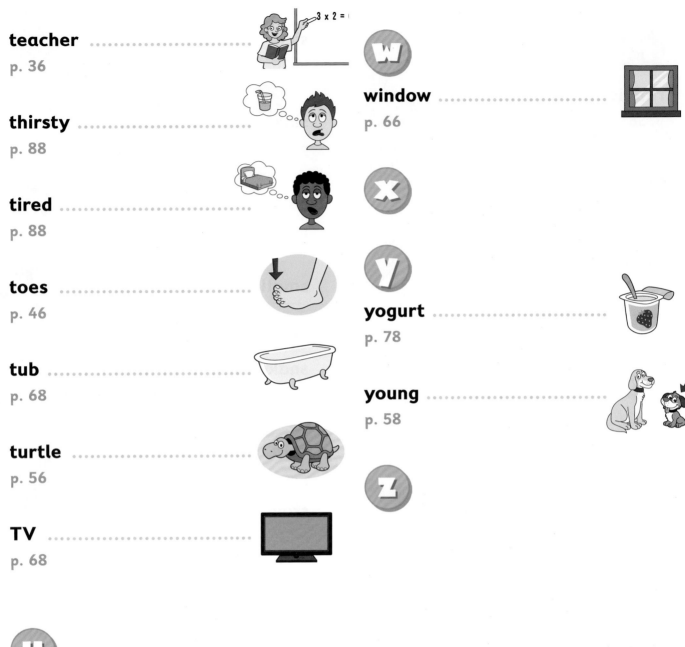

window
p. 66

yogurt
p. 78

young
p. 58

Acknowledgments

The Publishers would like to thank the following teachers for their suggestions and comments on this course:

Nurhan Deniz, Alejandra Juarez, Lara Ozer, Cynthia Xu, Basia Zarzycka

Jennifer Dobson, Anabel Higuera Gonzalez, Honorata Klosak, Dr Marianne Nikolov, Regina Ramalho

Asako Abe, JiEun Ahn, Nubia Isabel Albarracín, José Antonio Aranda Fuentes, Juritza Ardila, María del Carmen Ávila Tapia, Ernestina Baena, Marisela Bautista, Carmen Bautista, Norma Verónica Blanco, Suzette Bradford, Rose Brisbane, María Ernestina Bueno Rodríguez, María del Rosario Camargo Gómez, Maira Cantillo, Betsabé Cárdenas, María Cristina Castañeda, Carol Chen, Carrie Chen, Alice Chio, Tina Cho, Vicky Chung, Marcela Correa, Rosalinda Ponce de Leon, Betty Deng, Rhiannon Doherty, Esther Domínguez, Elizabeth Domínguez, Ren Dongmei, Gerardo Fernández, Catherine Gillis, Lois Gu, SoRa Han, Michelle He, María del Carmen Hernández, Suh Heui, Ryan Hillstead, JoJo Hong, Cindy Huang, Mie Inoue, Chiami Inoue, SoYun Jeong, Verónica Jiménez, Qi Jing, Sunshui Jing, Maiko Kainuma, YoungJin Kang, Chisato Kariya, Yoko Kato, Eriko Kawada, Sanae Kawamoto, Sarah Ker, Sheely Ker, Hyomin Kim, Lee Knight, Akiyo Kumazawa, JinJu Lee, Eunchae Lee, Jin-Yi Lee, Sharlene Liao, Yu Ya Link, Marcela Marluchi, Hilda Martínez Rosal, Alejandro Mateos Chávez, Cristina Medina Gómez, Bertha Elsi Méndez, Luz del Carmen Mercado, Ana Morales, Ana Estela Morales, Zita Morales Cruz, Shinano Murata, Junko Nishikawa, Sawako Ogawa, Ikuko Okada, Hiroko Okuno, Tomomi Owaki, Sayil Palacio Trejo, Rosa Lilia Paniagua, MiSook Park, SeonJeong Park, JoonYong Park, María Eugenia Pastrana, Silvia Santana Paulino, Dulce María Pineda, Rosalinda Ponce de León, Liliana Porras, María Elena Portugal, Yazmín Reyes, Diana Rivas Aguilar, Rosa Rivera Espinoza, Nayelli Guadalupe Rivera Martínez, Araceli Rivero Martínez, David Robin, Angélica Rodríguez, Leticia Santacruz Rodríguez, Silvia Santana Paulino, Kate Sato, Cassie Savoie, Mark Savoie, Yuki Scott, Yoshiko Shimoto, Jeehye Shin, MiYoung Song, Lisa Styles, Laura Sutton, Mayumi Tabuchi, Takako Takagi, Miriam Talonia, Yoshiko Tanaka, María Isabel Tenorio, Chioko Terui, José Francisco Trenado, Yasuko Tsujimoto, Elmer Usaguen, Hiroko Usami, Michael Valentine, José Javier Vargas, Nubia Margot Vargas, Guadalupe Vázquez, Norma Velázquez Gutiérrez, Ruth Marina Venegas, María Martha Villegas Rodríguez, Heidi Wang, Tomiko Watanabe, Jamie Wells, Susan Wu, Junko Yamaguchi, Dai Yang, Judy Yao, Yo Yo, Sally Yu, Mary Zhou, Rose Zhuang